7/10

contemporary asian

LIVING ROOMS

Chami Jotisalikorn and Karina Zabihi
photos by Luca Invernizzi Tettoni

PERIPLUS

Published by Periplus Editions, with
editorial offices at 130 Joo Seng Road,
#06-01, Singapore 368357

Copyright © 2004 Periplus Editions (HK) Ltd
Photos © 2004 Luca Invernizzi Tettoni

ISBN 0 7946 0179 0
Printed in Singapore

Distributed by:
North America, Latin America and Europe
Tuttle Publishing, 364 Innovation Drive,
North Clarendon, VT 05759-9436, USA
tel (802) 773 8930; fax (802) 773 6993
email: info@tuttlepublishing.com
www.tuttlepublishing.com

Asia Pacific
Berkeley Books Pte Ltd, 130 Joo Seng Road,
#06-01/03, Singapore 368357
tel (65) 6280 1330; fax (65) 6280 6290
email: inquiries@periplus.com.sg
www.periplus.com

Japan
Tuttle Publishing, Yaekari Building, 3F,
5-4-12 Osaki, Shinagawa-ku,
Tokyo 141-0032
tel (813) 5437 0171; fax (813) 5437 0755
email: tuttle-sales@gol.com

contemporary living rooms:
embracing the new global chic

From Bangkok to Bali, a relaxed new mood in contemporary living is steering the shapes and textures that form today's Asian living rooms. In luxury homes and design hotels across the region, seating is invitingly low-slung and laid back; cushions are deep and abundant; a heightened appreciation for air and light prevails. The new Asian living room beckons as a refuge from the jumbled cacophony of modern urban life. The new serenity to be found in living room spaces conveys the search for a sense of peace and order in our interior world, almost as if in response to the increasing unpredictability of the world beyond the walls of our home. Featured in the pages of this book are some of the most stylish living rooms across Southeast Asia, revealing how the formal elegance of pre-millennial living and entertaining has been replaced by a new desire for easy relaxation. The contemporary living room is a place that is meant to invite, not intimidate.

Traditionally, the key aspect of the tropical Asian living room is its relationship with the surrounding environment. Indeed, the distinction between western and tropical Asian living rooms lies in their opposing attitudes toward the external environment. In western homes, the living room is the space that shows the family's public face to visitors, a space that conveys status. One enters a European house through a formal entrance hall, then through doors leading into other rooms. The doors are functional, as they keep cold blasts of wintry air from chilling the rooms inside the house. It is no surprise then that the western living room centers on a hearth for warmth and comfort, enclosing people inside and protecting them from the harsher elements outside.

In the balmy climes of tropical Asia, the opposite rules prevail. In the mostly open-air lifestyles of Southeast Asia, there is hardly a formal front door, let alone any sort of formal entrance hall. The living room, or any communal social area in traditional Asian houses is open to the outdoors on all sides, or consists of a roofed pavilion with no walls, like the Indonesian *balé* or the Thai *sala*. The concept of living in tropical Asia embraces the outdoors as part of the living space, designed to incorporate cooling breezes and cross ventilation to ease the searing heat. The outdoor verandah is an important part of the tropical Asian living room too, as seen most clearly in the classic Thai stilt house, where the living room and verandah are one and the same. More modern examples show how the region's leading architects, including Geoffrey Bawa and Peter Muller, have understood this aspect of tropical Asian architecture: both architects pioneered the concept of incorporating the outdoors in contemporary architecture in their residential and hotel designs in Sri Lanka and Bali. In some traditional tropical Asian homes, the living and entertaining area opens up to a central garden so that the vista becomes part of the interior design element. Like the hearth in western living rooms, the garden in tropical Asian living rooms is the focal point of the room.

Given the region's fast-forward thrust from agricultural society to tech-savvy industrialization in recent decades—which in turn has spawned an insatiable thirst for all things western—what is the new Asian living room about? Air conditioning has eliminated the need to have an open living room for cooling and ventilation purposes, while the new mode of living in compact, confined apartments in congested cities has made the aircon one of the basic necessity of urban living. Yet in Southeast Asia, there remains an attempt to adhere to some mode of communication with the outdoors.

In modern city homes, this fascination with the outdoors not only harkens back to traditional living concepts, but has

a larger function of creating a buffer between the home and the bustling concrete city outside. The congestion of metropolitan living has instilled in urbanites a heightened desire for space, light, and wherever possible, a resort-like atmosphere that pays tribute to the outdoors. Many of the luxury homes in Bali, Singapore, Malaysia and Thailand featured in this book incorporate the outdoor courtyard, swimming pools and other water features into the living room, with the use of sliding doors, glass walls, or no walls at all, so that the living room appears one with the garden. Even highrise apartments try to introduce some outdoor elements into the living area, though in Bangkok and Singapore, the cityscape replaces the gardenscape—for example, in the lavish penthouse suites at The Metropolitan Bangkok, where the living rooms are dominated by vast, two-storey windows that attempt to swallow the entire sky in one gulp.

Within the walls (or lack of), a streamlined look is the desired look. Homeowners want interiors that are sharp, calm and clean-cut. Seen in its relationship to the outdoors, today's living rooms are a different reaction to the changed outdoor environment. As city life becomes more chaotic and stressful, homeowners and interior designers are making a deliberate choice to turn their homes into sanctuaries of calm in response to the chaos of modern living. The minimalist living room has become a symbol of serenity and an oasis for contemporary life.

What appears here between these covers is evidence of a new approach toward living room design that moves away from the classic Asian styles to embrace the international look in interior design. As Southeast Asia becomes increasingly influenced by global trends and the region's cities evolve into hubs of international travel, Asian design trends are leaning toward sophisticated sleekness—the minimalist, empty space and white-on-white palette that signifies a new high style.

What are the emerging furniture trends among designers and clients? What is apparent is the taste for European furniture including Minotti, Capellini, Rolf Benz and Ligne Roset. While it must be said that the look of contemporary furniture, with its focus on simplicity and minimal lines, gives an inescapable uniformity of shape to today's swarm of square-edged sofas, this in turn is balanced by a reliance on 20th century classics—for example, the Mies van der Rohe settee, the Corbusier chaise, the Barcelona chair, the Eames chair and the Arco lamp are some of the modern classics that serve

top left A bold blue cushion enhances the draw of this all-white room.
top right This elegant vase fashioned from blue glass is by Seiki Torige, whose works are now a fixture in the Asian design world.
above right Oriental antiques blend seamlessly with the symmetry of this modern living room.
right The graceful lines of the Emmemobili spring wenge chairs from Marquis give a contemporary feel to this open-plan living room.
far right Japanese-style seating adds the illusion of space in this living-cum-dining area.

to anchor the look of many contemporary living rooms. Even when these design icons aren't present in the original, modern Asian designers' re-interpretations of these classics reveal the impact these design canons have had on inspiring a new generation of 21st century designers. For example, in a condo living room in Bangkok (page 124), what appears to be an Arco lamp is a look-alike with a lampshade consisting of clusters of real silkworm cocoons, creating a soft glow with unexpected texture that reflects a new approach to lighting.

Yet in the midst of this insistent celebration of western chic, Southeast Asian homeowners still eschew a complete submission to artifice. They retain a sense of place by adding their personal choices of décor elements from Asia; paintings and sculptures by contemporary local artists and Asian artefacts that reflect the human instinct to forge an identity with the surrounding environment. The use of local materials also adds a distinctive Asian identity to the scene. In Thailand especially, local design firms such as Paanta and Yothaka are giving native organic materials new life by creating innovative new designs such as lamps made of wicker, loofah and silkworm cocoons, and chairs, cushions and vases made from water hyacinth to create new shapes and textures that are uniquely Asian in look and feel.

With furniture shapes and colors at their most minimal (white on white or black and white being the standard colors of the modern palette), the focus then falls on furnishing materials to add visual interest and textures. Leather, whether genuine or faux, is enjoying an all-time high in popularity as a

above Now enjoying new heights in popularity, leather is surfacing as the chosen material in cushions, flooring and furnishings. These patchwork leather side tables are by Paragon International in Thailand.
left This living room in a house in Singapore appears to be floating above the pool that runs the length of the room. Ultra-modern vases add an extra dimension of sophistication.

furnishing material. Leather tiles are the new ultra-luxe flooring material, and leather poufs and ottomans are making a comeback; the new look is the leather cube covered in mock croc, faux lizard, basket-weave leather strips, and buttery pleather. Leather area rugs have also broken through.

Leather cushions make their mark in various forms. In one Bangkok bachelor's home (page 90), all the sofas (Minotti, of course) in the entire house are padded with leather cushions from Fendi. Cushions come in plaited leather squares, distressed leather rectangles, furry goatskin, shiny tanned leather, and patchwork suede. In many homes, leather is a material favored by male homeowners as a look that spells slick masculine sophistication.

When it comes to textiles, "nubby" is the new buzzword in fabrics. The most cutting-edge living rooms sport cushions that are fuzzy, knotted, furry, or hairy with threads. In the Modern Contemporary Suite in Bangkok's Sky Villas, an armchair and matching cushion are upholstered in fuzzy black faux fur seemingly skinned from a teddy bear (page 36).

Though Italian furniture and barely-there colors dominate the new look in Asian living rooms, what distinguishes the new Asian living room from being just a carbon copy of its western counterpart is the subtle presence of the Asian aesthetic. The particular look of east-meets-west is perhaps best embodied in the work of Singaporean interior designer Kathryn Kng, designer of The Metropolitan Bangkok and other luxury resorts in the region. It is a minimalist, soft-toned palette that combines the latest in European furniture design with singular accents from one or two artfully chosen Asian antiques which lend the perfect balance to the new fusion look. For example, in the penthouse suites at The Metropolitan Bangkok (page 42–43), the key furnishings are cutting-edge

left The colors of this painting by Canadian artist Jonathan Forrest provided the inspiration for the interior design of this spacious house in Singapore.
above Bright red flowers add a striking note in this otherwise honey-colored open-plan living and dining area in an apartment in Singapore.

Italian sofas and lamps, while the Asian accents come from an oriental-style coffee table, a bamboo opium bed and hand-embroidered pillows from India. A similar aesthetic is seen in a Singapore residence designed by Eco-id Architects (pages 22–23). Here the architects designed an international-style minimalist space and the homeowners created an exquisite balance between the white-on-white western furniture with their Asian art collection of Khmer pots and Chinese paintings.

Modern Asian art is emerging in a big way in interior décor —partly due to the increased frequency and scope of travel that is now an aspect of life. Artworks by Bali-based American painters Symon and Tracy Hamer and Thai artist Tawul Praman, and the fantastic glass creations by Japanese glass sculptor Seiki Torige are found in the region's most style-conscious homes. Homes now have gallery spaces in hallways, entrance foyers, stairway landings—on top of living rooms—to show-case art collections.

The taste for a minimalist aesthetic in today's living rooms shows that contemporary Asian living embraces the new look of global chic. Combined with their passion for cutting-edge Italian furniture and lighting, Asian homeowners take pride in sporting an unmistakably local, sophisticated design aesthetic that proclaims the region has switched on to contemporary cool. The new Asian living room reflects the way homeown-ers embrace the whole world, celebrating the best in modern international design with the distinctive personal touches that mark where they have come from or where they are living. It's an international attitude that reflects the way we live now.

above Paired with a simple arrangement of grass, this Hugh Chevalier leather armchair makes a thoroughly modern statement.
left Warm orange walls and a richly woven tribal rug evoke the colors and patterns of Morocco in this Bangkok home. Balanced with low-lying coffee table and seating, the scene embodies the new look of the international living room.

in ship shape   An unconventional triangle shape and glass walls on all sides
suggest expansive freedom in this weekend home built on a golf course in Thailand,
conceived by Bangkok architect Robert Boughey of Boughey and Associates.

left Juicy fruit colors and funky shapes add quirky charm to the vast white space. A whimsical orange chair in the shape of a hand and a banana-yellow pouf were sourced from local shops, while the pointy Rolf Benz sofas echo the home's triangle shape. A vibrant scarlet painting in the living room energizes the entire space. The painting of a monk's fan is by well-known Thai artist Tawul Praman.

above The view from the living room shows the triangle corner of the house ending in an airy pointed terrace, complete with a Jacuzzi pool. Perfectly positioned for entertaining, the custom-made circular bar relieves the severe lines of the structure. Glass walls and sliding glass doors open the interior space to the golf course, giving the occupants a luxurious sense of endless greenery.

above The upstairs sitting area becomes a meditation room with the simple addition of a mattress and throw pillows. The paintings depict a series of monks' fans by Thai artist Tawul Praman, who is famous for his renditions of Buddhist themes.
left The view from the meditation room shows how the pointed upper terrace of the triangle house overlooks the golf course. Glass walls on all sides flood the house with sunlight, creating a delightfully airy atmosphere.

above It feels like a ship's deck on the terrace, furnished with matching triangular chairs—perfect for watching the sunset.
right A spectacular spiral staircase made of white terrazzo offers dramatic passage in an ivory tower.

a simple plan This modern Bangkok residence is a picture of chic simplicity, thanks to Vitoon Kunalungkarn of IAW, designer of the distinctive minimalist boutiques for Thai fashion vanguard label Greyhound and its eponymous trendy cafes.

above A rustic wooden side table displays earthy collectibles such as handwoven baskets and the carved wooden balls and bowls from Habitat. The lattice screen also provides shade, eliminating the need for curtains.

left Textured stone walls provide an elegant backdrop for a Minotti chair paired with ceramic vases from a local market.

opposite Vitoon has a genius for creating stylish spaces without blowing the budget, focusing on light and space to create interiors of stark elegance. The living room has a calming effect with a mix of Italian furniture from Minotti, ceramic vases from Anyroom and Habitat and an antique Burmese wooden coffee table that doubles as a storage chest. Lattice screens are an ingenuous way to display art—paintings hung on both sides can be seen from the inside and outside of the house.

spatial awareness The immediate impression on entering this house in Singapore designed by Lim Ai Tiong of LATO Design is one of sweeping open spaces enhanced by the double-volume passageway.

right "The owner's brief was to have a spacious interior with minimum maintenance," says Lim Ai Tiong and this bright and airy living area encapsulates that brief. The corner window and two horizontal windows above and below the television add to the brightness of the otherwise austere space decorated with the very minimalist black leather sofas and chrome and glass coffee table from Home Couture.
left The dropped ceilings in teak add another dimension to the open space as Lim Ai Tiong explains. "As the living, dining and open dry kitchen are one uninterrupted space, I needed to create a sense of distinction and intimate sense of space between the functional areas without affecting the spacious quality."

above Leading from the front door is this 10-meter long passageway. The timber flooring and columns draw the eye to the soaring end wall illuminated by the skylight above. The wall is made from cement boards, the sizes and holes of which were meticulously worked out.
right Vibrant red accessories from The Link add character to this fabulous long wall bench.
left The juxtaposition of vertical and horizontal elements and contrasting textures and materials is what makes this dining and living space interesting. The staircase strikes an austere, industrial note that is softened by the teak wood detailing. A compressed marble floor reinforces the sensation of abundant space.

eastern joys and western styles In Serene and Lars Sorensen's home
in Singapore designed by RichardHo Architects, the influence of eastern and
western beauty exudes warmth and cosiness.

left The wooden swing-louvered doors infuse a contemporary look to this living and entertaining space, which, as Serene puts it, combines antique and modern together "to preserve fond memories of old pieces and to create new memories with the modern ones."

above The magnificent views onto the lush greenery in front of the house and the tall ceilings are what Serene appreciates most about this living room, where she can indulge in her love of tea ceremonies. Her affection for oriental furniture is evident in the day bed from The Life Shop and coffee table from Tomlinson's.

chequered charm Amidst the spectacular architecture of the Tirtha Uluwatu wedding resort in Bali designed by Glenn Parker of Grounds Kent Architects, the comfortable lounge encourages guests to unwind before the ceremony.

left The interiors of the resort were done by Ratina Moegiono of PT Alindi Kyati Praya. The brief was for a clean contemporary look—formal and elegant yet with a relaxed air. All the furniture was custom made by the interior design company.

above A beautiful four-block coffee table created by the design team takes pride of place in the living room. Fabrics from Europe and Hong Kong add warmth and character while mother-of-pearl inlaid trays make for an unusual art feature.

rock star chic   The brief given to the Nine Squares design team for the interiors
of this villa at Downtown Apartments in Bali was "to make it look fit for a rock star!
Very cool, stylish and luxurious whilst not conforming to any conservative ideals."

left Even rock stars need to work sometimes! This living room cleverly incorporates a built-in desk unit and sleek wooden chair from Urban Icon for when office duties call.

below French artist Veronique Aonzo's graffiti artwork adds a radical chic touch at the entrance to the villa.

opposite Cool blue is the predominant color in this superstar living room with its individualistic details throughout. A splash of bright yellow is provided by Veronique Aonzo's "Love" canvas. All the interior furnishings and fittings were imported from designers in Australia, including the leather sofa from Arthur G and the blue spangly standard lamp and the four-pronged vase from Melbourne-based Room Interior Products. The overall effect is indelibly modern and ultimately stylish.

urban groove An offshoot of the trendy Greyhound Café group, the To Die For restaurant is conceived and designed by Bangkok style guru Bhanu Ingkawat in the fashion of a New York loft; hence the raw brick walls and edgy urban glamor.

above Outdoor seating takes the form of a four-poster day bed with thick mattresses and mountains of nubby cushions for maximum chill effect.

right and far right New wave wall lamps take lighting to the level of art installation.
opposite The scene spells urban cool, with furry ottomans, a low, curvy chair and a well-worn leather sofa in the restaurant's sitting area. Italian lighting adds the high-style element.

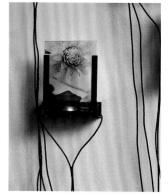

single space set up Condo living can often mean condensed living and when kitchen, living and dining are all-in-one, the challenge is to create a space that is easy to use, as in this Bangkok condo designed by DWP Cityspace for Sky Villas.

above Overhead lamps help define the dining space as a separate area from the living room area. A consistent theme of wood surfaces and decorative balls made of wicker and shells keeps the overall feeling warm and organic.

right A small dining table looks bigger with the help of a glass top while upholstered chairs add luxe. A textured wood wall and surprising fabrics such as the black teddy-bear textured arm-chair and cushions provide the modern touches that give the room its contemporary feel.

designing from the inside out "It creates a perfect reflection in the swimming pool at night, like a mini Taj Mahal," says Richard North-Lewis of the outdoor living room he designed and renovated in his home in Bali.

above The contrast between cool whites and a traditional Alang Alang roof is both soothing and visually stunning. The stainless steel downlighting is custom made by Paul Turner Lighting in Bali.

left Richard North-Lewis, who owns Stoneworks, wanted to redesign his outdoor living space. "It all started with wanting a modern sofa," he says. "So I designed the space from the inside out, with everything matching the sofa! To enhance this, I decided to use limestone and stainless steel."

right Seiki Torige's blue glass vase adds a splash of color in the otherwise white and soft grays of the living space.

far right Four limestone blocks make for unusual tables. The limestone from West Java, which Richard used for the blocks, floor and pillars, "absorbs the colors of the sun all day."

the bold and the beautiful "We love the impact and drama of the room,"
say Andy and Michele Wilkinson of this audaciously dramatic living space in their
condominium in Singapore designed by K2LD Architects.

left and far right "The living room is sculptural," Michele says. "There are minimal pieces but each one makes a strong statement to create a sense of drama." What started the "red" theme were the two Wink chairs from Cassina and the two Kick tables, which stand out against the custom-made dark gray sofa in the sunken lounge. The result is a room that is ultra-modern and super-sexy.

above Chinese artist Zhu Wei's painting has incredible impact. "We really love his artwork because he has a great sense of color and texture, a simple but dramatic style and wonderful sense of humor," says Michele. The couple re-sprayed their Compass speakers to match the room's overall red theme. The leather Canta chair designed by Toshiyuki Kita for Cassina is the ultimate in modern furniture art.

top Michele's love of cows is much in evidence in "Annabel," the cow that Andy bought for her in Hong Kong.

high on style   A minimalist, east-meets-west aesthetic sets the theme in the penthouse suites at The Metropolitan Bangkok. The look, created by Kathryn Kng, balances
the latest in Italian design with new interpretations of classic Asian accessories.

above Southeast Asian hill tribe
accessories take on new life as
décor objects in these elegant
pieces from the Club 21 Shop
in The Metropolitan.
left The creamy vanilla Italian
sofa by Patricia Urguilo is balanced by the chocolate tones
of a bamboo-top coffee table in
the style of a traditional Chinese
opium bed. The sequined cushions, imported from India, are
from the hotel's Club 21 Shop.

right The duplex suite gets a
dose of high drama from double-decker windows draped in
silk from Jim Thompson.

executive chic Designed by Carolyn Corogin of C2 Studio, this living room in the Siri Sathorn Bangkok service apartments embodies contemporary casual with a masculine edge for its mostly businessmen clientele.

above The look is relaxed and cool, conceived as a welcoming retreat from the noisy city. The structural pillar in front of the window created an awkward and seemingly useless niche, but the designer installed a cushiony window seat, transforming the niche into an inviting nest for secluded reading or napping.

right The furnishings were custom designed for comfort and sophistication. The structural pillar was mirrored to add greater dimension, with a recessed top to create the illusion of a higher ceiling. The ceiling edges were recessed for the same effect. The painting is by Bali-based American painter Symon.

soothing sophistication   "Calming and uncluttered" is how the owners describe the spacious living room in their house in Singapore. The interior designer was Janet McGlennon and the architect was Kevin Tan of aKTa-rchitects.

above These three wooden monks are among the owners' favorite pieces. "We love them because they look so serene," they say.

left The simple symmetry of a dark console table, porcelain pot and artwork presents a delightful introduction to the rest of the living room.

opposite The owners wanted soothing neutral colors to dominate in the living space. Janet introduced rich splashes of colors like purple for the sofa to give a plush feel to the room. The contemporary look of the room contrasts pleasingly with the artwork and Asian coffee table custom made by Apsara.

double-decker drama A duplex penthouse in Bangkok takes full advantage of the cityscape with two-storey windows and two-tiered sitting rooms that offer rooms with a view. The formal sitting room for entertaining guests is on the lower level.

above The upstairs sitting room is on a mezzanine overlooking the main sitting room below, and serves as a TV room outside the bedroom for relaxed lounging.
left The low-slung green leather Italian armchair is designed for comfort, whereas the partition is designed to evoke the architecture of Thai temples, with vertical recesses that let in light. The wall provides a perfect backdrop to a vase from Italy.
right The artwork on the landing is by Marc Rambeau, a French artist whose paintings of Buddha were inspired by his traveling experiences in China.

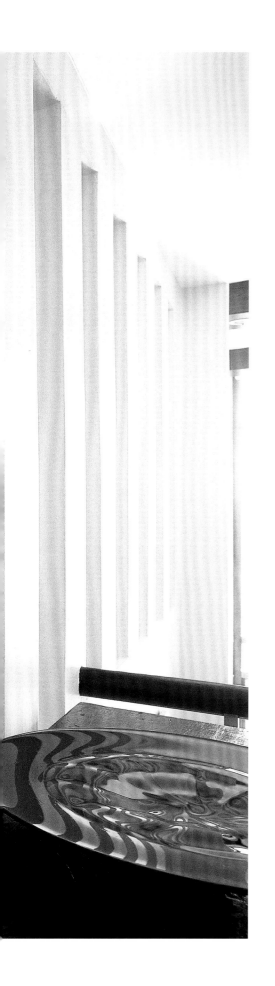

above The gold-leaf work in the entrance hall gives a modern Asian welcome to all who enter. The artwork was custom made by a professor of fine arts using materials from Japan.

left The open staircase, framed by the double-height ceiling, is the best place to admire the dramatic cityscape.

opposite From the U-shaped Italian sofa by Dema, guests are allowed a bird's eye penthouse view. The facing cabinet is a 19th century Xing Dynasty artifact from Shanxi. The Neolithic vase is from Central China and the coffee table, from Lotus Lifestyle Gallery in Bangkok.

sky retreat   This duplex penthouse was conceived and designed by the owner as a pristine aerie retreat far removed from the bustle of Bangkok. The focus is on a clean-cut modern look, using European furniture mixed with modern Asian accents.

above In the upstairs sitting room, white Italian chairs paired with stainless steel Swiss lamps give the space the stylish look of a hip hotel.

right Minimal spaces need no more than a few textures and shapes to add sophistication, such as these glossy shell patterned vases and lacquer bowls from Lamont Contemporary.

left The stunning crystal stupa by Bali-based glass artist Seiki Torige is displayed to dramatic effect beneath the glass and stainless steel stairway designed by the owner. In the living room area, a classic Asian-style table is paired with convertible Italian sofas from Ligne Roset.

luxe glam The elegance of this open-plan living space in a Singapore apartment designed by Calvin Sim of Eco-id Architects lies in the use of rich fabrics and timeless classic colors in dark tones and hues.

left The living room defines elegance with the clean lines of the Hugh Chevalier armchairs providing a dramatic contrast to the antique Buddha head. Eschewing the trend for blinds, the designer opted for drapes. "As the look we were trying to achieve was luxury with a 'glam' undertone, we felt silk curtains were appropriate," she says. She also designed the coffee table and the Tibetan silk rug that she had custom made in Nepal. A painting by Thai artist Nattee provides a focal point to the space.

above The apartment, in fact, has two living rooms. This smaller study, which benefits from a large window stretching the length of the room, employs the same muted palette but with lighter tones. "We added taupe fabric panels to the walls to give the room a sense of luxury," says Lim Siew Hui, Head of Interior Design at Eco-id Design Consultancy who created the interiors. The artwork on the wall was done by Calvin's father.

attuned to nature One of the hallmarks of the houses designed by Kevin Tan of aKTa-rchitects is the interaction between the outside and the inside. This house in Singapore exudes openness and offers a true communion with nature.

left The brief the owners gave to Kevin Tan was for a "modern tropical" house. The tropical look is achieved with the grand, high-pitched teak ceiling and *balau* wood pillars that frame the open-plan living room. The modern element is introduced by contemporary yet classical furniture from B&B and armchairs from Fendi. The owners are enthusiastic art collectors and among their large collection is Srihadi Soedarsono's "Dancer's Dialogue" which makes a strong and immediate visual impact on the space. What they love best about this room is the "warmth of the teak wood enhanced by the limestone floor, high ceiling and views of the garden."

above Behind the main sitting room is this hallway that leads to the staircase and the floors above. The owners have taken advantage of the recess in the wall to create a tranquil, private extra seating area, reminiscent of those in an art gallery. Well-placed artwork adds definition to the space.

artful living The owners' large and important collection of contemporary Canadian art and the open-plan space gave kzdesigns the inspiration for the interiors of this house in Singapore, where everything revolved around the colors of the collection.

above A contemporary painting by Canadian artist Jonathan Forrest contrasts yet complements a traditional planter chair from Lim's Art and Living.
left A custom-made acrylic plinth half-filled with potash is an imaginative means of displaying this wrought-iron sculpture made by the owners' son.

The open living room is a perfect blend of the old and the new, the oriental and the modern. Four cubes from Space, used as variable coffee tables, contrast well with the owners' much-loved leather sofas and the armchairs which were re-upholstered to reflect the colors of Jonathan Forrest's painting, seen on the previous pages.

pitched perfect The relationship between the environment and architecture forms an important part of the work of GM architects. This villa in Bali is a perfect example of the inside–outside feel that defines modern tropical living.

left The sloping wooden roof is undoubtedly one of the most striking features of the living room in the villa and makes a definite and bold statement— open as it is on one side to the garden and pond beyond. The organic contours of the space are further enhanced by the use of tactile and soft-toned stone. The color scheme of gentle golds, creams and natural wood reinforces the warm and tranquil mood of the room.

above A secluded, private patio with its own miniature garden is the perfect place for early breakfast or afternoon tea. Cool white walls and stone floors create a harmonious balance between the exteriors and interiors.

inspired elegance For the owners of this large house in Singapore, designed by Sim Boon Yang of Eco-id Architects, it was important for the living room to "feel like it's in a garden" and act as a conduit to the rest of the house—"like a big foyer."

above The natural tones of earth and soil against a simple white palette inspired the color scheme for this restful and elegant living room. The owners are avid collectors of art and antiques. For them, "the art in the house is essentially a collection of fond memories. The modern furniture plays a practical role and somehow they fused well together," they say. All the furniture was custom made for this exceptionally large room. Eartharts, a stone supplier, helped the owners find the right marble for the coffee table. "As the table is really very simple, it is the natural beauty of the marble that made all the difference," they say.

left One wall in the living room opens up completely to the pool and the garden. "We sit in the living room often with our feet in the water—a very relaxed environment," say the owners. A recess set into the wall dividing the living and dining areas is the perfect location for their beautiful collection of Khmer pots, and on the adjacent wall is a painting entitled "Goldfishes" by Tan Swie Hian, which the owners bought for their son.

eye candy   The combination of vintage '50s chairs and tables and European
picture frames juxtaposed with Asian textile accents is a cross-cultural mix-and-
match that signifies a new global chic.

left Low-slung seating and chubby cushions set the tone for drawn-out meals in the restaurant's Gossip Room, enhanced by the inviting textures of soft silks and velvets.

top Beribboned birdcages and exuberant plastic flowers give the Gossip Room the girly kitsch of a teenager's bedroom.
above This plastic mini-lamp (circa 1970s) is a campy alternative to table-top candle light.

tribal beat The exotic colors and tribal flavor in this Bangkok residence were inspired by the days the owner spent in North Africa. A single strong color is used in the living room to create a backdrop for a collection of tribal and contemporary art.

above Sleek black Italian chairs flank a painting by contemporary Malaccan artist Charles Cham. Plastic floor lamps from Giles Caffier cast a moody magenta glow. The wooden sculpture is by Thai artist Khun Saiyart.
left The spectacular head, a Bamana marionette over 100 years old, was imported from Central Africa. A painting by Thai artist Maitree Pharahom contrasts dramatically with a yellow Philippe Starck chair.

opposite Warm orange walls evoke the colors of northwest Africa, anchored by the deep, earthy tones of a Moroccan tribal rug. The seats are molded into the wall, custom designed by the owner to mimic the seating of a Moroccan home, complete with cushions covered in traditional black and white Indonesian fabric. The colored glass bottles on the table are made of Murano glass from Venice. An Indonesian *balé* in the garden beyond offers Asian-style outdoor seating.

The owners transformed part of the living room into a gallery space showcasing both tribal and contemporary works. Taking center stage is an Indonesian rice pounder from Bali, modified into a modern candle stand. Two African Bobo tribal masks from Burkino Fasso flank a Mao painting from a series by Chinese political pop artist Zhao Cong Sheng. The wooden posts at the far end support pillars normally found in Balinese courtyards. Tribal rugs from Morocco adorn the floor.

blue in bali The outdoor living space in architect Glenn Parker's Seseh Serasi villa in Bali strikes an impressive note with the use of cool white stone and touches of blue against the traditional Alang Alang roof.

right A simple rattan wicker chair by Peter Bunter Design hits just the right note and complements the terrazzo floors. A bright blue cushion adds a fine contrast.
below The open, free-standing steps are like a staircase to heaven. Palimanan stepping-stones inlaid into concrete provide interesting detailing.
opposite The overall impression in the open-air living room is one of intimate grandeur. The beauty of the terrazzo stone floor is shown off to the best advantage against the wood pillars and Alang Alang roof. Stone steps lead to the upstairs area and extended walls made from Paras Yogya blocks shelter the bedrooms and bathrooms at the back of the living space. A basic white palette enhances the clean lines of the stone.

a sanctuary of style "Minimalism and simplicity prevail in the living and dining area, which is a common space that we all share," say the owners of this house in Singapore designed by Sim Boon Yang of Eco-id Architects.

left "A room for all seasons," is how the owners describe this fantastic all-glass living room. A carefully chosen combination of fabric, leather and wood "gives a nice texture and feel to the entire room."

top The ambience of the living space constantly changes. In the moonlight, the room gives the illusion of floating above ground. **above** Dividing the car porch from the house are these 18 blocks of cement, chipped at the edges to resemble stone pillars.

mood living   By experimenting with layers, open spaces and a miniature garden in the interior of this Singapore apartment, Geraldine Archer of Mara Miri has created a modern yet welcoming home for a young couple.

left Geraldine's main consideration was how to "enlarge" the living area. "The space in the living room has a difficult layout as the L-shape is quite narrow and is part of the 'corridor' to the rest of the flat," she says. She also likes to bring nature into the home, and has incorporated an indoor garden which has a "way of making the eye settle on this feature almost instantly."

above By building a platform in the room, Geraldine has effectively divided the space and created a comfortable seating area for television viewing and relaxing. The dominant shades of brilliant blue in the sofa, together with the large plant pot and accessories from Orientation offset the wood columns and decking and add to the new Asian feel the owners were after.

revealing layers "The site and landscape helped a lot in providing a background of colors for the living space," explains Benny Cheng of space_craft, who designed this elegant yet modern home in Singapore.

left Against a basic white, there is an "evident layering of tones and colors in terms of space," says Benny. "More is revealed as you enter the home and you are greeted by not only space but the combination of shades and light." The iconic Arco lamp and furniture from Space complete the look of effortless grace.

above A growing trend in Asia is for ponds and water features in the home. In this house, as Benny explains, "there was a drop in levels in the existing site. Short of making stairs through the whole width we thought it might be a good idea to bring the water connection in. It also mirrors the skylight above."

relaxed fusion With the mixed influences of Italian architects Sotssas Associati,
the design tastes of a Japanese wife and an English husband, the effect of the living
room in this house in Singapore is highly individual.

above The vibrant blues and reds in this porcelain dish make for a striking contrast against the glass coffee table.

right One of the beauties of this house is the intricate detailing on the doors and staircase. The asymmetrical lines of the stairwell breathe light and modernity into the space.

left This room demonstrates how the modern and the old can tastefully co-exist. Much of the owners' antiques were bought in Hong Kong, like the 120-year-old Chinese gown which reflects the colors of the Tai Ping carpet. The collection of bronze Indian children's toys contrasts well with the custom-made white sofas from Abitex Designs.

transparent modern living   What the owners love about their home in Kuala Lumpur, designed by Ernesto Bedmar of Bedmar & Shi, is the fact that "even though it is a very modern structure, it is not cold. It is a very warm, inviting space."

When it came to the design of their home, the owners wanted something contemporary but "not overpowering." The open spaces round the house play an important part in the design. "My husband is an avid gardener and the garden is a very integral part of our lives," says the owner. The black granite used in the interiors add warmth to the house and contrast well with the *balau* wood of the pillars in the portico. The inspired choice of furniture—the soft gray sofa and mocha leather armchairs from Moie—reflects and enhances the natural hues and tones of the structural material employed.

above The very essence of the house is transparency with a natural fluidity between the spaces. This granite wall accommodates the door to the dining room, while the outdoor portico leads to the living area beyond.
left One of the most interesting features of this house is how the owners have combined a super-modern look with unusual Indian artefacts and antiques. These two columns, which the owners sourced in India, provide a dramatic effect against the purity of the sleek Roman blinds while also echoing the natural environment beyond.

opposite The living and dining areas create one seamless continuous space. A small pond near the dining area brings the garden into the room. The rough black granite walls provide a great contrast to the smooth white in the background and the boat masthead from Kerala.

retro remodeled What first attracted architect Lillian Tay to this late 1960s house in Petaling Jaya in Kuala Lumpur was the lofty living room. After a series of renovations, the house appears more transparent yet remains faithful to the original design.

left Lillian's house is filled with interesting artwork. The papier mâché sculpture of a dolphin (called a *duyung*) was made by German artist Ruth Gilberger from old '70s floral wallpaper. The staircase which Lillian put in to replace the original period '60s spiral staircase leads to the bedrooms and library. The blue wall came about because she wanted a color that would recede against the overall white walls to create a greater sense of spaciousness in the central living and dining space. "The soft blue reminds me of sun-faded walls in Mediterranean villages," she says.
below Translucent gold candle holders add immediate warmth to the space.
opposite Low, modern furniture accentuates the double-height pitched ceiling of painted plywood panels typical of the '60s and '70s. Lillian buys artwork "simply to have them round me to look at and think about." Three paintings—two of which are by Malaysian artist Yau Bee Ling—add a poignant touch.

the future is fun Eschewing the traditional layout of sofa and coffee table, kzdesigns opted for pieces that make a more "futuristic" statement in this house in Singapore designed by HYLA Architects.

left In order to give a more spacious feel to the ground floor of the house, architect Han Loke Kwang demolished the wall that originally divided the living and dining rooms. The "T" wood column and console introduce a strong sculptural form. Keeping the dining table small enlarges the space while a full-height glass wall leading to the kitchen directs the eye to the new extension at the back of the house. The light box used as a table and distinctive low plastic armchairs—all from X•TRA Living—infuse the space with a singularly modern feel.

above The sharp definition of X•TRA Living's black and white armchairs, cushions and organic vases provide a dramatic contrast to the pale wood of the storage unit and wall that leads to the front entrance.

opening act This Bangkok residence is an example of an increasingly popular approach to city living—the removal of walls lets in space, natural sunlight and garden views, giving the home a resort-like atmosphere.

above Wide sofas by Minotti and low tables from Casa Milano make an inviting place to relax and enjoy the view. The cushions are handwoven from dried river reeds and raffia and were hand-made by villagers in remote areas of South Africa. A painting by Australian artist Todd Hunter hangs in an alcove.

right The existing walls in this house were replaced by sliding glass walls leading out to the pool and grounds. When the space is expansive, large pieces are called for to keep the propor-tions in balance. Minotti sofas are plumped up with extra large cushions in knitted leather from Nicole Farhi Home. Artworks, such as the large painting on wood pulp by Australian artist Robin Metcalf, are similarly scaled to suit the high ceilings. The sculpture is by Shona Nunan, another Australian artist, and is displayed on a stunning alu-minum pedestal from Mauro Mori in Milan.

a chocolate box "Contemporary living with modern Asian highlights" is how Index Design describes the living room of this apartment at The Equatorial in Singapore. The rich tones used by the designers make the space inviting.

left The warmth of chocolate tones combined with a soft neutral palette brings sensuality to the living space. A teak slatted screen separates the living and dining areas while allowing light to circulate. The room plays on duality with two deep armchairs, two dark wood side tables and a low, round coffee table all custom made by Index Design. The relatively low height of the furniture accentuates the space.

above A small space should not be overwhelmed by large pieces of furniture. Here, the custom-made wall bench gives extra seating but also acts as a vehicle for this singular square wood sculpture from Index Design's private collection. Soft lighting generates a soothing glow in the room. A local artist was commissioned to create the honey-toned painting which adds to the serenity of the space.

lines of light   When the owners of this house in Singapore approached HYLA
Architects to design their home, the emphasis was to create an open space
dominated by clean lines and lots of natural light.

left The "floating" staircase against the party wall enhances the height of the living and dining space. When it came to decorating the space, the owners chose pieces that "looked classic and would stand the test of time," such as the mustard Frigetto Cubo from Limited Edition, the dark rug from Mod.Living and the two Frog chairs designed by Lissoni for Living Divano at Cream. A painting by Ann Healey standing on an acrylic base picks up the colors and tones used elsewhere in the space.

above These glass doors that pull all the way back to reveal the front patio area further accentuate the openness of the space. The color scheme of the room is comfortable and welcoming. This fun and funky Squeeze Bench designed by Patrick Chia provides "the only curves in an area otherwise dominated by straight lines," say the owners. "It makes a really dramatic counterpoint."

the soft touch   Against the magnificent backdrop of Singapore's cityscape, this luxurious, open-plan living room at The Equatorial apartments created by Index Design offers "opulent comfort within an urban oasis."

left Achille Castiglioni's famous Arco lamp accentuates the sleek glass-topped coffee table from Le Mercier.
right The neutral palette of the living room is enhanced by dollops of rich chocolate colors in the foot stools and the fake fur throw. The floor-to-ceiling windows are framed by Orsbone and Little curtains. As Angelena Chan of Index Design explains, "These drapes define the concept of 'self-pampering' at home that blinds would not give." A mirrored wall reflects the open-plan dining area beyond, enhancing the space.
below These unusual white light boxes from Index Design's private collection add a very modern touch to the by-and-large classic feel of the room.

a fusion of forms   The free-flowing living area of Elizabeth MacLachlan and David Skillen's Singapore apartment designed by Sim Boon Yang of Ecoi-id Architects is a picture-perfect blend of oriental antiques and contemporary design.

above On entering the apartment, the eye is immediately drawn to the enormous tapestry and the assortment of antique pots which allow the space to breathe.
left The owners' exceptional collection of Burmese pots and Japanese archery bows make for an outstanding display.
right All the furniture was custom made. One of the most interesting pieces is the fabric coffee table which provides extra seating areas for guests and also softens the hard surfaces of stone, glass and marble.

left Elizabeth calls this living room on the second floor their "mucking around" room. It embodies all the necessities that make up a snug family niche, like big comfy sofas and chairs, a television and books—displayed on a metal book rack from Blue Canopy—with the family antiques and artefacts that define the rest of the home. Large floor-to-ceiling windows offer an amazing view over the harbor, while at night, soft lighting enhances the cosiness of the space.

above The original staircase in the apartment was a heavy concrete winding staircase. "We wanted the steps to 'float' upstairs and decided on a glass banister to enhance that effect," says Elizabeth. "The main point was to open up the entrance so your first view was the actual living room rather than the transitional space of a stairway upstairs," she adds. On the wall are two old Chinese doors from a temple in Singapore the couple found along Balestier Road. The junk dealer (who had bought the whole temple) was initially reluctant to sell the doors until the couple had signed a contract giving him first refusal to buy them back!

leather living This Bangkok loft apartment designed by owners Michael Palmer and Vichien Chansevikul also functions as a showroom and testing ground for the luxurious leather home décor items from their company, Paragon International.

above The apartment's design theme is the square, as seen in the square grid window treatment and square niche shelving. These side tables, designed by the owners, were inspired by the apartment's grid motif theme and are made of leather patchwork. **left** Lush, sand-colored lizard skin gives a contemporary twist to a simple console table. A trio of fresh cabbages makes a simple and stunning floral display. **opposite** A set of leather altar tables with a matching leather candle holder pays homage to a painting of Buddha by Thai artist Tawul Praman. The niche shelves display an installation by the same artist, depicting miniature Buddhist monks and fans. Wheels are attached to the leather poufs in black woven leather and sea-green lizard skin to allow for easy movement. The sofa cushions covers are made of leather—butter-soft suede on the far end and braided leather in the foreground.

it's all about balance In the brief given to Raymond Seow of Free Space Intent, the owners of this two-storey HDB apartment in Singapore wanted him to redesign their home so it had a "modern resort" look to it.

left Along one entire wall, Raymond custom made a television console incorporating a glass light box and laminate-base materials used elsewhere in the apartment. For him, it is "the mix of greenery with modern materials and furniture that gives this apartment the balance," he says.

above The green glass of the console unit mirrors the overall color scheme of the apartment—natural greens and white with glass and cement. A simple Buddha head adds an eastern element to the modern flat.

left To create a more spacious and contemporary apartment for his clients, Raymond demolished the existing floor and wall tiles, overlaid laminate on the floors, and re-plastered and re-tiled the walls. Separating the living room and dining spaces is this space-age hallway that doubles as a storage unit. This passageway has proven to be a unique feature of the apartment. Having the minimal amount of furniture enhances the space and draws the eye to the balcony that now forms part of the living area.

right Rather than the tried-and-tested standard or ceiling lights, Raymond thought it "would be cool to have concealed lighting beneath the floor."

scarlet fever How do you convey a cultural identity through the use of simple color? A bold and brilliant red color scheme shouts out Sino Modern style at The Rice Mill Chinese restaurant at the Marriott Resort & Spa Bangkok.

above Plump silk cushions in red and yellow squares extend the walls' geometric color scheme.
left Bright vermilion walls and contemporary paintings show a new way to express a Chinese mood. Effusive color can become overwhelming when left to run riot, but in this elegant room the potency of the vibrant yellows and reds is subtly diffused by containing the brilliant colors in a strictly balanced grid of rect-angles. Flanking the sofa, a pair of lamps with classic vase bases reflects the old Chinese belief in pairing items for balance.

arty ambiance Upstairs sitting rooms are the less showy, more private spaces where homeowners retreat from entertaining. The sitting room of this Bangkok home is where the owner can kick back and contemplate his abstract art collection.

left This roomy landing leading to the sitting room is transformed from transit corridor to gallery space with the owner's collection of Australian contemporary art. These works by artist Ronnie Tjanpitjinpa depict aboriginal themes. The figurines are by Australian artist Shona Nunan, who has exhibited around the world and was commissioned to provide sculptures for Chek Lap Kok Airport in Hong Kong.
opposite High ceilings topped by a skylight give a lofty allure to the sitting room. The focus is on relaxation—with low-slung, laid-back seating inviting the occupants to lean back and just chill. The sofa and armchair are from B&B Italia and the wood and metal coffee table by Minotti. The painting depicts dreaming, and is by George Tjungurrayi, an Australian aboriginal artist.

modeled for the man about town   In the living room of this Singapore apartment created by kzdesigns for Reuter's man, Mike Tyldesley, the emphasis is on stylish, state-of-the art entertaining.

above These night-light holders from The Touch House of Art and Design offset the Asian day bed from Barang Barang.
right A chrome and slate coffee table is the perfect foil for this fun car ashtray. Square PVC poufs allow for extra seating while a central light box of PVC and acrylic casts a soft glow over the room (all pieces by kzdesigns).
left The designer created bright orange acrylic light boxes to add a dash of color to the living room. The specially designed stereo cabinet houses all Mike's hi-fi equipment. Black-and-white jazz photographs by UK-based Caroline Emmett complete the masculine look of the room.

subtlety and simplicity   By retaining the shell but completely redeveloping the interiors of this house in Singapore, architect Michael Cu Fua has fashioned an adaptable family living space with a hint of bohemian modern.

The main colors in the house are black and white, "representing the earth and sky for me," says Michael. He found the four office chairs—which he re-upholstered in Australian leather—in Chinatown. An unusual white flower vase from Cream sits in the center of the coffee table, another of Michael's designs. The bohemian atmosphere of the living room is enhanced by the absence of a television set, making it a truly interactive space, while the large canvas by Eric Chan softens its monochromatic quality. What Michael likes most about the living area is "the flexibility of opening up all the sliding doors from the master bedroom to the car porch. I end up having a very big volume of space to entertain in," he says. Billowing swathes of white muslin divide the living and sleeping areas, and add an innate sensuality to the home.

playing with light & white Designer Albano Daminato is drawn to modernist buildings of the mid '60s for "their devotion to rigorous spatial planning." For him, this apartment he redesigned in Singapore is "a sanctuary from the world outside."

above By opening the folding glass doors, the dining and living areas are transformed into one "large living salon." The wicker stools—another of Albano's designs—were originally created for the Pierside restaurant in Singapore.

left Sori Yanagi's famous butterfly stool in ash has an organic, timeless appeal.

opposite The living room is at-ease chic; minimal in its design yet speaking volumes about the designer's impeccable taste. There is an immediate appeal about crisp white roller blinds, while the long fitted bookshelf Albano designed is perfect in its sleek simplicity. The dark sofa with back cabinet is a classic Danish design by Hans Wegner. Eric Chan's moody painting provides the one element of color.

balinese grandeur "A place so seductive that you don't want to move, dramatic and warm enough to laze around with two or party away with 40," is how Danielle Mahon describes Ylang Ylang, the villa she designed in Bali.

left An old tree branch becomes a sculpture. Tiny frangipani buds add a quixotic touch to this natural arrangement.
opposite The living and dining area is completely open on all sides. Sheer drapes framing the entrance columns waft gently in the breeze. For Danielle, the house is "a very personal interpretation of western and Asian architecture, a theater of modern decadence with a Balinese spirit."

above With her passion for travel, art and architecture, Danielle's inspiration for the "beach house" she designed for herself and her husband, Mike, came naturally from her "trips down memory lane." Seen from the sweeping gallery above, the sizable living room benefits from large items of furniture, all of which were custom made in Mike and Danielle's lifestyle company, Chair N Tango.

a soothing space When it came to the design of this spacious family holiday home in Bali, architect Cheong Yew Kuan wanted to depart from the traditional-style villa yet still retain certain Asian aspects like the openness and roof lines.

above Resin flooring and a concrete wall place this villa firmly in the modern context while the white drill-covered, custom-made day beds give the outdoor living area a "soothing, peaceful feel," according to the owner. The coffee table, fashioned from a solid piece of teak, is typical of the furniture made by Bali-based design company Aulia.

left The landscaping by Trevor Hillier is an integral part of the design of this glorious villa. When it came to the furniture for this part of the living space, the owner opted for large day beds. "From the bigness of the space I knew I wanted Chinese ones," she says. The orange and red silk cushions are influenced by Tibetan colors.

male model　Sleek black and white leather defines the new style vocabulary for the modern urban man. This Bangkok condo in Sky Villas epitomizes the contemporary look of sophisticated comfort, as interpreted by the design firm DWP Cityspace.

left White leather gives a crisp look to the classic black Wassily chair, while the plush leather sofa is plumped up with goatskin cushions. The mirrored pillar between the two windows adds depth to the narrow room, and also shows how blue neon cove lighting lends a nightclub glamor to the slick space.

above Extra wide, extra low metal garden chairs are the new look in outdoor seating and give plenty of perch space for a coffee break on a lazy afternoon. The balcony overlooks Chong Non Si intersection on Sathorn Road in Bangkok's vibrant central business district.

a sensitive approach Designed by Dutch architect Joost Van Grieken, this private villa near Ubud in Bali demonstrates a harmony with the surrounding environment through its perceptive architectural style.

above The bold and sensual painting is in marked contrast to the otherwise neutral color palette of this space. *Bengkerai* wood used for the door lends solidity to the whole, while the stone *objets* and console table present elegant and linear forms that resonate with the overall design of the villa.

right Spectacular views from the open-air living space impart a serenity to the villa. By using a controlled choice of materials, the architect has enhanced the transparency of the design. The roof introduces a local element while the combination of grays and reds envelop the villa with an aura of warmth.

lap of luxury The impeccable lines of modern European classics and the marriage of lush leathers with perfectly proportioned furniture give enduring appeal to this living room designed by Singaporean firm APC for Bangkok's Domus condominiums.

above The subdued glow from
a tubular Italian glass lamp from
the Orrizonte shop in Bangkok
dispenses with regulation shades
and makes the lamp a high-tech
design item, to be displayed next
to paintings and décor pieces.
left You can't go wrong when
the furniture is Italian. Minotti
sofa and leather chairs are balanced with 20th century design
icons—a Mies van der Rohe
chaise longue and an Arco lamp.
A low table and a faux fur rug
bring the look of the living room
into the new millennium.

organic appeal Highrise living is imparted a down-to-earth ambience, thanks to the new trends in organic furniture design in this Bangkok living room designed by DWP Cityspace for Sky Villas.

above Old materials take on new shapes such as this funky coffee table made of wicker from the Paanta shop in Bangkok.

left A water hyacinth cushion from the Ayodhya shop in Bangkok is both visually striking and environmentally friendly. The new use of water hyacinth plants as popular and stylish furnishing and décor items helps keep these plants from choking Thai waterways.

opposite The arching lamp may have a familiar shape, but the unusual use of Thai silkworm cocoons gives lighting a soft, funky new look.

The authors would like to express their thanks to the following people who gave their kind support during the production of this book:

BALI
Anjarini Kencahyati, Arthur Chondros at Downtown Apartments, Cheong Yew Kwan, Daniel Ellaway of Nine Squares, Fredo Taffin, Gill Wilson, Glenn Parker, Jaya Ibrahim, Mike and Danielle Mahon and Richard North-Lewis of Stoneworks.

Cheong Yew Kwan tel: (62) 361 197 8777, email: area@indo.net.id

Fredo Taffin Espace Concept, 250 Beddington Rd, Noosa Heads Doonan, 4562 QLD Australia, www.espaceconcept.net

Glenn Parker email: gpai@indosat.net.id

GM email: gmarc@tiscalinet.it

Jenggala Keramik Jln Uluwatu II, Jimbaran Bali, tel: (62) 361 703 311, www.jenggala-bali.com

Joost van Grieken email: joost@idola.net.id

Nine Squares email: info@ninesquares.com, www.ninesquares.com

Pesamuan Jln Pungutan 25, Sanur Bali, www.pesamuan-bali.com

Paul Turner email: bilptl@dps.centrin.net.id

PT Alindi Kyati Praya email: alindi@indosat.net.id

Seiki Torige Galeri Esok Lusa, Jl Raya Basangkasa 47, Seminyak Kuta, 80361, tel/fax: (62) 361 735 262, email: gundul@eksadata.com

Stoneworks email: sabitadesign@telkom.net, www.stoneworksbali.com

Veronique Aonzo email: mymonamour@hotmail.com

MALAYSIA
Lillian Tay of Veritas Architects.

Veritas Architects 148 Jln Ampang, Kuala Lumpur 50450, tel: (03) 2162 2300, www.veritas.com.my

SINGAPORE
Kevin Tan of aKTa-rchitects, Ernesto Bedmar of Bedmar & Shi, Jean Khoo of City Developments, Michael Cu Fua of Cu Fua Associates, Sim Boon Yang and Calvin Sim of Eco-id Architects, Raymond Seow of Free Space Intent, Richard Ho of RichardHo Architects, Han Loke Kwang and Hilary Lo of HYLA Architects, Angelena Chan of Index Design, Ko Shiou Hee and Romain Destremau of K2LD Architects, Lim Ai Tiong of LATO Design, Geri Archer of Mara Miri and Benny Cheng of space_craft.

Abitex Designs 290 Orchard Rd #04-09/11 Paragon, S'pore 238859, tel: (65) 6338 7789

Ann Healey www.annhealey.com

aKTa-rchitects 25 Seah St #05-01, S'pore 188381, tel: (65) 6333 4331, www.akta.com.sg

Barang Barang #01-35 Great World City, S'pore 237994, tel: (65) 6738 0133

Bedmar & Shi 12A Keong Saik Rd, S'pore 089119, tel: (65) 6227 7117, email: bedmar.shi@pacific.net.sg

Blue Canopy 391 Orchard Rd, #02-12G Ngee Ann City, S'pore 238872, tel: (65) 6734 3505

Caroline Emmett email: af2c@hotmail.com

Club 21 Gallery Four Seasons Hotel, #01-07/8, 190 Orchard Blvd, S'pore 248646, tel: (65) 6887 5451, www.clubtwentyone.com

Cream 5 Purvis St, #01-01–3, S'pore 188584, tel: (65) 6333 9115, email: creamhome@pacific.net.sg

Cu Fua Associates 43B Dickson Rd, S'pore 209518, tel: (65) 6291 1172, www.cufua.com

Eco-id Architects 11 Stamford Rd, #04-06, Capitol Bldg, S'pore 178884, tel: (65) 6337 5119, email: ecoid@pacific.net.sg

Fluv Floral Stylists 66 Club St, S'pore 069440, tel: (65) 6536 8806, www.fluv.com.sg

Free Space Intent 80 Nicoll Hwy #01-84, S'pore 188836, tel: (65) 6334 2150, www.freespace.com.sg

Home Couture 114 Lavender St, #01-00 Hock Seng Bldg, S'pore 338729, tel: (65) 6298 7328

HYLA Architects 47 Ann Siang Rd #02-01, S'pore 069720, tel: (65) 6324 2488, www.hyla.com.sg

Index Design 15-A Purvis St, S'pore 188594, tel: (65) 6220 1002, fax: (65) 6334 7262

Janet McGlennon Interiors 129 Devonshire Rd, S'pore 239886, tel: (65) 6733 5580, fax: (65) 6733 5117

K2LD Architects 136 Bukit Timah Rd, S'pore 229838, tel: (65) 6738 7277, www.K2LD.com

kzdesigns tel/fax:(65) 6836 3365, email: rokasing@singnet.com.sg, www.kzdesigns.com

LATO Design 520 Balestier Rd, #04-00 Unit 7 Leong On Bldg, S'pore 329853, tel: (65) 6475 7571, fax: (65) 6476 7571

Le Mercier 65 Mohammad Sultan Rd, S'pore 239003, tel: (65) 6734 2561

Lifestorey Great World City #02-33D, 1 Kim Seng Parade, S'pore 237994, tel: (65) 6732 7362, www.lifestorey.com

The Life Shop 290 Orchard Rd #04-30 Paragon, S'pore 238859, tel: (65) 6732 1719, www.thelifeshop.com

Lim's Arts and Living 211 Holland Ave, Holland Rd Shopping Centre #02-01, S'pore 278967, tel: (65) 6467 1300

MARA MIRI email: gnrptltd@singnet.com.sg

Mod.Living 331 North Bridge Rd, #02-01/08 Odeon Towers, S'pore 188720, tel: (65) 6336 2286, www.modliving.com.sg

Moie 123 Penang Rd, 01-13 Regency House, S'pore 238465, tel: (65) 6235 2260

Orientation #01-03 Stamford House, 39 Stamford Rd, S'pore 178885, tel: (65) 6338 1125, www.orientation-home.com

Quedos Home Works 61 Stamford Rd, #01-02 Stamford Court, S'pore 178892, tel: (65) 6338 1171, email: sales@quedoshomeworks.com, www.quedoshomeworks.com

RichardHo Architects 691 East Coast Rd, S'pore 459057, tel: (65) 6446 4811

Sottsass Associati email: sottsass@sottsass.it, www.sottsass.it

space_craft 324 River Valley Rd, S'pore 238356, tel: (65) 6333 3108, www.spacecraft.com.sg

Space Furniture Millenia Walk Level 2, 9 Raffles Blvd, S'pore 039596, tel: (65) 6415 0000

The Life Shop Raffles City Shopping Centre #03-26, S'pore 179103, tel: (65) 6338 3998, www.thelifeshop.com

The Link Boutique # 01-10 Palais Renaissance, 390 Orchard Rd, S'pore 238871, tel: (65) 6737 7503, www.TheLink.com.sg

The Touch House of Art and Design 38 Bukit Pasoh Rd, S'pore 089852, tel: (65) 6325 4990, www.thetouch.com.sg

V.Hive Home Interiors 109 North Bridge Rd, #02-37/41 Funan the IT Mall, S'pore 179097, tel: (65) 6338 9348

X•TRA Living 9 Penang Road, #02-01 Park Mall, S'pore 238459, tel: (65) 6339 4664, www.xtra.com.sg

THAILAND
Arthur Napolitano, Brian Renaud, Carolyn Corogin of C2 Studio, Chananun Theeravanvilai of Chime Design, Debbie Thio, Delia Oakins of Carpediem Galleries, H Ernest Lee, Jacques Baume, Kingkaew Puengjesada and Kittima Kritiyachotipakorn of Golden Land Property Development, Laura Herne of Outlaurs, Pornsri Rojmeta of To Die For, Rika Dila, Stephen Bennett, Supranee Taecharungroj of The Metropolitan Bangkok, Sylvain Guisetti, Vichien Chansevikul and Michael Palmer.

Abacus Design 144 (off) Soi Siripot, Sukhumvit 81, Bangkok 10250, tel: (662) 742 4571 6/331 9966, fax: (662) 332 8649, email: abacus@ji-net.com

Anyroom 4th Floor Siam Discovery Center, Bangkok 10330, tel: (662) 658 0583, www.anyroom.com

C2 Studio The Prime Bldg, Level 15, Suites B&C, 24 Sukhumvit 21, Bangkok 10110, tel: (662) 260 4243, email: Carolyn@c2studio.net

Carpediem Galleries #1B-1 Ruam Rudee Bldg, 566 Ploenchit Rd, Bangkok 10330, tel: (662) 250 0408, email: deliaok@loxinfo.co.th

Club 21 Shop at The Metropolitan Bangkok, 27 South Sathorn Rd, Bangkok 10120, tel: (662) 625 3333, fax: (662) 625 3300, email: info.bkk @metropolitan.como.bz, www.metropolitan.como.bz

Domus (sales office) 18th Floor Lake Rajada Complex, 193/72 Rajadapisek Rd, Bangkok 10110, tel: (662) 661 9300, fax: (662) 661 9331, email: bkk_ressales@cbre.com, www.domus.co.th

DWP Cityspace The Dusit Thani Building, Level 11, 946 Rama 4 Rd, Bangkok 10550, tel: (662) 267 3939, fax: (662) 267 3949, email: nijaya.i@dwpartnership.com, www.dwpartnership.com

Habitat 989 Siam Discovery Center, 4th Floor, Rm 418-420, Rama 1 Rd, Bangkok 10330, tel: (662) 658 0400, fax: (662) 658 0401, www.habitat.net

IAW Soi Panich-Anan Sukhumvit 71, Bangkok 10110, tel: (662) 713 1237, email: iawbkk@loxinfo.co.th

Sky Villas The Ascott Bangkok, 187 South Sathorn Rd, Bangkok 10120, tel: (662) 676 8888, www.goldenlandplc.com